The Aquinas Lecture, 1967

RELIGION
AND
EMPIRICISM

Under the Auspices of the
Wisconsin-Alpha Chapter of Phi Sigma Tau

BL
51
S64
R3

By

JOHN E. SMITH, D.D., PH.D.

MARQUETTE UNIVERSITY PRESS
MILWAUKEE
1967

Library of Congress Catalog Number 67-20684

PRINTED
IN
U.S.A.

Prefatory

The Wisconsin-Alpha Chapter of Phi Sigma Tau, the National Honor Society for Philosophy at Marquette University, each year invites a scholar to deliver a lecture in honor of St. Thomas Aquinas whose feast day is March 7. These lectures are customarily given on the first or second Sunday of March.

The 1967 Aquinas Lecture *Religion and Empiricism* was delivered on March 5 in the Peter A. Brooks Memorial Union by Professor John E. Smith, professor of philosophy, Yale University.

Professor Smith was born on May 27, 1921, in Brooklyn, New York. He earned the A.B. at Columbia University in 1942; the B.D. at Union Theological Seminary in 1945; the Ph.D. at Columbia in 1948.

He began his teaching career at Vassar College and from 1946 to 1952 was Instructor and then Assistant Professor at Barnard College, Columbia University. He joined the Yale faculty in 1952 as Visiting

Assistant Professor and in 1953 joined the regular philosophy faculty at Yale, becoming Associate Professor in 1955 and full Professor in 1959.

Professor Smith was a Morse Fellow at the University of Heidelberg in 1955-56. In 1960 he was the Dudleian Lecturer— one of the oldest distinguished lectureships in the United States, having been founded by a member of the Harvard College class of 1696. In 1963 Professor Smith was the Suarez Lecturer at Fordham University and received the Honorary LL.D. at the University of Notre Dame in 1964.

Professor Smith's publications include: *The Spirit of American Philosophy*, New York: Oxford University Press, 1963; *Reason and God*, New Haven: Yale University Press; a critical edition of Jonathan Edwards' *Treatise Concerning Religious Affections*, New Haven: Yale University Press, 1959; translation of R. Kroner's *Kants Weltanschauung*, Chicago: Chicago University Press, 1956; *Royce's Social Infinite*, Indianapolis: Bobbs-Merrill Co.,

Inc., 1950; articles in many philosophical and theological journals.

To these publications Phi Sigma Tau is pleased to add: *Religion and Empiricism.*

Religion and Empiricism

In one of those generalizations that are not entirely true, but are too instructive to be false, a recent writer has suggested that while the ancient Greek philosophers were fascinated chiefly by the cosmos, and the major philosophers of the Middle Ages concerned themselves primarily with God, the persistent topic of modern philosophy for the past two and a half centuries has been man, his nature and conduct. It was not a philosopher but the 18th century poet, Alexander Pope, who expressed this concern in a pointed way when he declared that "the proper study of mankind is man." One of the most important consequences of this modern drift in philosophical interest has been the appeal to *experience* which made itself felt throughout the major philosophies of Enlightenment, and found expression in the writings of such diverse thinkers as Locke, Kant, Rousseau and Hume.

The fundamental idea behind the new appeal to experience was that man can encounter the world and himself directly, and thus attain, in the form of the experience that results, a touchstone of truth and reality. Being contemporaneous with the data presented, or as we might now express it, "seeing for yourself," became the ultimate criterion for judgment. Both Locke and Kant were fond of contrasting those who beg their thoughts from others, with those who dare to attend to their own experience and draw conclusions from it. According to the new doctrine, past beliefs and conclusions, traditions and claims both to knowledge and to power, however ancient or revered, must meet the test of experience. The contact with reality, frequently understood as the sensible present, was made the judge and master over all the deliverances of the past.

The fundamental idea of experience as both the substance of philosophical thought and the criterion of its validity, proved itself to be a persistent one. The idea and the doctrines through which it found expression, came to be developed in several different directions so that, in addition to what I shall call "classical empiricism" — the characteristic position of Locke and, in a different way, of Hume— other forms of the appeal to experience have appeared in response to new problems and interests. Logical empiricism, linguistic empiricism, pragmatic empiricism and radical empiricism are the names for these new philosophical standpoints. Despite profound differences between them, all are committed to the proposition that something called *experience* is, to paraphrase Dewey, the ultimate arbiter of all questions of fact and existence.

This history of the empirical philosophies forms a chapter in the history of thought which has its own importance; I wish, however, to single out for special attention a more limited topic, the question of the implications of the appeal to experience for religion, and especially the bearing of that appeal on the problem of God. For religion, which is at once so intimately connected with the nature of man

and with the problems of metaphysics,
could not well have remained unaffected
by developments that resulted in establish-
ing the experience of the individual person
as the touchstone of meaning, of knowledge, and of existence. Prior to the emerg-
ence of classical empiricism in the late 17th
and early 18th century, western religious
thought had become, through long associ-
ation, deeply involved in the major metaphysical traditions that had been established in the ancient world. Platonic and
Aristotelian ontologies were taken for
granted by the great theologians and even
the Reformers who criticized metaphysics
had to come to terms with Christianity's
long history of metaphysical theology. Insofar as the new approach through experience called into question many doctrines
of past ontology—including the possibility
of the theory of Being itself—the bearing
of the philosophy of experience on religion
cannot help but be a topic of primary importance. The development, moreover, of
new forms of empiricism in contemporary

thought underlines that importance in the present.

The issue as it confronts us is not merely the challenge of new ideas, nor does it mean offering a defense of traditional beliefs in the face of empiricism considered as inimical to religion; more important than either is the question of the role of experience in religion, and the resources made available by a philosophy of experience for raising and resolving the perennial problem of God. For it seems that so personal and individual an affair as religion undoubtedly is, can scarcely be expected to live without experience, and yet when we consider some of the claims that have been made in the name of experience it may seem that religion cannot live with it. With these considerations in mind, I propose to discuss the bearings on religion of three forms of the appeal to experience —classical empiricism, linguistic empiricism and pragmatic or radical empiricism —with the ultimate aim of assessing the validity of this appeal in the critical treatment of the religious questions.

Thus far I have used the expression "appeal to experience" and the expression "empiricism" as if they were synonymous. I hear at once the objection that experience itself is one thing, and empiricism is quite another. Experience, it will be said, is the record of what we encounter, find, suffer, discover, in our transactions with the world, while empiricism is the technical term for a philosophical doctrine dealing with the ground of knowledge and existence. Just as we can surely see without geometry, the objector may continue, we can just as surely experience without empiricism. The objection I fully accept, as long as the problem to which it points is understood and taken seriously. The appeal to experience has never been, and in my view cannot be, philosophically naive. The appeal to experience, that is to say, cannot be advanced apart from a general theory—whether explicitly asserted or not —of the nature or general shape of experience, involving at the same time some specifications as to what is to count as experience, what is to be included or excluded

from it. This point has often been over-
looked, especially when it it supposed that
appealing to experience as a criterion for
judging a given philosophical interpretation, is a simple appeal to a domain of neutral and pure "fact" over against supposed-
ly biased and differentially oriented "theories." This view of the matter is mistaken;
the appeal to experience is always an appeal to experience understood or interpreted in some way. And even if we agree
that experience is too complex and com-
prehensive to be described adequately in
terms of one predicate, such as sense, feeling, or immediacy, it does not follow that
appealing to experience is an appeal that
can be made entirely apart from a theory
as to what sort of thing is to count as an
experience. Even Dewey, who saw this
point more clearly than any other philosopher, could not avoid a *general* description
of experience as such. Instead, however,
of trying to identify experience with one
quality, he defined it functionally in terms
of *method*.

In view of the fact that experience,

even in its richest and most complex conception, is not self-interpreting, the appeal to experience must always be critical, which means that it is an appeal to experience in some way understood. It is for this reason that there are so many "empiricisms." We must not suppose that the existence of this plurality implies the illegitimate or illusory character of the appeal to experience; on the contrary, despite the existence of different empiricisms, philosophies which take experience seriously continue to stand in sharp contrast to those which do not. Whereas, for example, Dewey and Russell disagreed on almost every philosophical issue, their concern for experience clearly distinguishes their views from those of rationalists like Leibniz or McTaggart or the mathematical logicians in which that concern is largely absent. The main difference is that the empirical approach means the return of every conceptual scheme to the experiential level from which it arose, while the mark of rationalism is that a conceptual scheme, once launched, gains autonomy within itself so that the criterion of its validity is made to reside in the conceptual scheme itself, its consistency and coherence. The experiential philosophy begins with experience and, in the end, returns to experience again; rationalism may set out from experience but, once it is secure in its rational analysis, there is no return.

I. Religion and Classical Empiricism

Anyone who considers the treatment of religion and especially the discussion of God found in the writings of Locke and Hume, cannot fail to notice a singular fact, namely, that these thinkers did not carry their empiricism to its logical conclusion. They hesitated when they reached the idea of God and, in order to deal with the problem, they were forced to borrow from the doctrines of the rationalists they were criticizing. Locke, as I shall suggest, was the more consistent of the two chiefly, because his conception of experience was richer, but even Hume, who was more uncompromising in his application of the criterion of sense than Locke, fell back in

the end on "natural belief" when he approached the idea of God. Hume did not,
like some contemporary "empiricists" said
to be his heirs, declare the idea of God
meaningless on the ground that it is, literally, devoid of sense. The point is crucial
and bears further consideration. If experience is identified with what is present to
the senses, simply and without qualifica-
tion, the problem of transcendence is re-
solved at one stroke: there is no transcendence and experience, so understood, becomes irrelevant to religion. The question
is, of course, whether experience can be
identified with the sensible present and
nothing else. The classical empiricists
came close to adopting that position, but
their hesitation in applying this doctrine
to the analysis of the idea of God suggests
that they entertained doubts.

In response to his own question concerning the source of the materials consti-
tuting human reason and knowledge,
Locke said, "To this I answer, in one word,
EXPERIENCE."[1] Within the scope of experience, Locke included *sensation*, or sim-

ple ideas derived from our senses, and *re-flection*, or simple ideas apprehended by the mind in attending to its own operations. It is important to notice that, in company with many of his contemporaries, Locke thought of experience as *basically* composed of *simple* elements that are particular in nature. Complex things are the result of the mind's operation on the simples. The inclusion of the ideas of reflection within experience was of decisive importance; for through them Locke was able to provide experiential content for the idea of God as the Supreme, Eternal and Omnipotent Being.

According to Locke's anatomy of the idea of God, we arrive at this notion by applying the idea of infinity[2] or by "enlarging" certain ideas derived from our own experience — existence, duration, knowledge, power, pleasure, etc.—until we reach the complex idea of God. The idea of infinity, Locke insisted, is derived from sense when we consider the addition of parts— spaces, times, numbers — to each other without limit. As a result of such repeti-

Ilimitado

tion, we reach the idea of the boundless[3] and in so doing we become aware of our *power* to carry on the additive process without end; the awareness of this power represents the material content of the idea of infinity. This idea is the key to understanding the idea of God; by means of the enlarging process we remove from the ideas derived from our own experience that finitude which would make them inadequate for expressing the divine nature.

Locke did not believe that we adequately understood the complex idea of God formed by the operation of the mind, but it is clear that he entertained no doubts about our knowledge of the divine existence. That existence is known through a cosmological type argument which is heavily dependent on the rationalist tradition as represented especially by Descartes. Despite his appeal to experience, Locke does not suppose that our knowledge is restricted by the limits of sensation. On the contrary, in his analysis of our knowledge of existence[4] it is claimed that we have in fact a three-fold knowledge; we know our own existence by intuition, the existence of material things by sensation, and the existence of God by demonstration. This demonstration starts from knowledge of our own existence and employs the principle of causality to reach God. We move from the simple idea of existence, gained by reflection on ourselves, to the divine existence. Whatever has its being from another is said to have its knowledge and its power from that other. To be the cause of man's existence and that of sensible things, God must be eternal, all-knowing and all-powerful. Locke rejected the ontological argument on the ground that not all men have the requisite idea of God, and that every starting point other than our own existence is inferior in certainty. By retaining the principle of causality or sufficient reason and by including within experience the ideas of reflection, Locke was able to maintain knowledge of what transcends the bounds of sense.

There are, of course, many questions to be raised about Locke's view; I shall mention but two in order not to obscure the main point which is that one of the founders of the western empirical tradition in philosophy did *not* consistently attempt to confine experience to the limits of sensation. Although Locke was much less phenomenalistic than Hume, he nevertheless helped to establish the conception of experience as a "mental product" immediately present to an individual mind. This conception has continued to give credence to the objections of those who want to ignore experience on the ground that it is a merely "subjective" affair. Moreover, Locke's disconnection of "abstract" or universal ideas from existence taken as that which is utterly singular, has helped to contribute to the belief that existence itself is unintelligible.[5] He gave support to the dogma, long associated with empiricism, that universal or necessary truth does not refer to existence, while particular affirmations or negations that would not be certain if universalized, do apply to existence. The implication is that existence has to do only with the "accidental" union or separation of elements; intelligibility means necessity and necessity is separate from existence. Existence is not intelligible. Here a larger problem emerges; if the dogma is accepted, an exception must be made with respect to God. The divine existence cannot be understood as the union or separation of the accidental, hence either God is the great exception to the system, or the dogma that necessity excludes existence must be given up. Locke retained the dogma and made God an exception.

Hume presents the position of classical empiricism in a more radical way than Locke, a way that is at once more phenomenalistic and skeptical. There is no need to trace out the familiar details of his theory of human experience and knowledge, nor to identify his own position on the religious question expressed in the *Dialogues Concerning Natural Religion*. The central point is that, despite Hume's insistence on a basis for experience in sense impressions, and his generally skeptical view of human knowledge as radically conditioned by man's nature, he maintained a theistic position, if not as a matter of "knowledge" in the strict sense, at least as a form of "natural belief" which human beings cannot avoid adopting. And, in fairness to Hume, it should be pointed out that insofar as his view of experience does include *belief,* experience must be more extensive than sense perception, for belief is a matter of judgment which is an affair of mind and does not take place in the level of simple perception.

The appeal to experience in Hume did not mean a sweeping denial in every sense of what transcends the horizon of experience. Experts are not of one mind in interpreting his theism. Whether one sees it as a failure to carry out his empiricism consistently, or as a valid consequence of a view of experience that is richer than he has generally been given credit for, the fact remains that Hume was not prepared to condemn the idea of God—at least in the sense of the Supreme Being of Deism —as devoid of significance. In the end, Hume's position must be seen as somewhat ambiguous. On the one hand, there is his

very strong and widely quoted statement
to be found at the end of the *Inquiry:*

> If we take in our hand any volume; of
> divinity or school metaphysics, for in-
> stance; let us ask, *Does it contain any ab-*
> *stract reasoning concerning quantity or*
> *number?* No. *Does it contain any experi-*
> *mental reasoning concerning matter of fact*
> *and existence?* No. Commit it then to the
> flames: for it can contain nothing but
> sophistry and illusion.[6]

Applied consistently, these principles
would preclude Hume's own theism, for
the analogy upon which it is based and
the reasoning from the finite to its cause
or ground which it requires, do not fit into
the category of "relations of ideas" or
"matters of fact." On the critical or skeptical side of his thought, Hume despaired
of finding intelligible grounds for religious
belief and consequently he argued against
depending on "metaphysical" support for
religion.

On the other hand, if Hume's view of
experience is interpreted so as to include
the activity of judgment required for the

formation of natural belief, and if, moreover, the content of that natural belief concerning religion is taken seriously, Hume's
theism has a basis both in experience and
in human nature and is not devoid of reason. Whatever may be the final truth about
Hume's own belief, the point of major importance for our inquiry is that, while the
position maintained by the classical empiricists involved major changes in the traditional approaches to God, their appeal
to experience, supplemented by elements
taken over from the rationalists, still al-
lowed them to reach theistic conclusions.
Despite the fact that recent forms of "empiricism" which deny the meaningfulness
of the term "God" are regarded by their
proponents as derivative from Hume and
Locke, it remains the case that these philosophers denied neither the meaningfulness nor the existence of God. The curious
fact is that Hume was concerned ultimate-
ly with the question of the divine nature.
Instead of discussing whether the term
"God" is meaningful, Hume wanted to discover what meaning we must attach to it.

Consequently, in the *Dialogues,* Hume began with the explicit statement that, while
there are problems in expressing clearly
what we mean by the term "God", the existence ("being") of God is not in question.[7]

II. Religion and Linguistic Empiricism[8]

Any discussion of the contemporary
form of empiricism based on the analysis
of language begins with the extreme form
of empiricism known as logical empiricism or positivism, even if, as is undoubtedly the case, very few philosophers today
would explicitly defend the position as
originally stated either by A. J. Ayer or the
Viennese positivists. According to logical
empiricism, we approach philosophical
questions by first considering the *meaningfulness* of the terms in which both questions and solutions are couched. For this
purpose a general criterion of meaning
was required; it was supplied in the first
instance by the well known verifiability
principle, according to which a proposition is meaningful if and only if it is (in

principle) capable of *empirical* confirma-
tion or disconfirmation. And by "empirical" was meant that the item referred to
in the proposition is present to a percipient
in and through sense perception. Experience, in this view, was identified with the
singular, atomic perception having a date,
a place and a percipient attached. Experience became no more than a flash of quality, something like a patch of red per-
ceived by Otto at 5:18 PM on June 12,
1900 plus, of course, many more qualifiers
aimed at making the perception absolute-
ly unique. The severely abstract and limited character of "experience" so conceived, is obvious. Experience has neither
depth nor transitional character; it is con-
fined to the surface of the datum and it is
a static picture or record of a tiny extract
taken from a natural habitat that is con-
veniently ignored. Positivism greatly reduced the scope of experience in compari-
son with the view held by Locke and
Hume, even if, as I shall claim, the classical view itself must come in for criticism as
too restricted when compared with the

richer theory of experience put forth by
the pragmatic philosophers.

The positivist meaning criterion when
applied in its strongest form to the sentences of metaphysics, theology and ethics
chiefly, eliminated them at one stroke from
the sphere of the cognitively meaningful.
Such sentences were either declared meaningless or assigned to the sphere of what
was called "emotive" meaning by which
was understood either that they *express*
feelings, or *indicate the existence of* feelings in the one uttering the sentence. The
main critique of metaphysical and theological discourse about God resulting from
positivism has been well expressed by
Ayer:

> . . . if "god" is a metaphysical term, then it
> cannot be even probable that a god exists.
> For to say that "God exists" is to make a
> metaphysical utterance which cannot be
> either true or false. And by the same cri-
> terion, no sentence which purports to de-
> scribe the nature of a transcendent god
> can possess any literal significance . . . it is
> characteristic of an agnostic to hold that

the existence of a god is a possibility in which there is no good reason either to believe or disbelieve; and it is characteristic of an atheist to hold that it is at least probable that no god exists. And our view that all utterances about the nature of god are nonsensical, so far from being identical with, or even lending any support to, either of these familiar contentions, is actually incompatible with them. For if the assertion that there is a god is nonsensical, then the atheist's assertion that there is no god is equally nonsensical, since it is only a significant proposition that can be significantly contradicted.[9]

From this perspective, there can be no intelligent argument about God because the key term in this discussion is "nonsensical" which means, in accordance with the verifiability criterion of meaning, that the term "God" does not denote a sensible reality. The prior application of the meaning criterion keeps the question of God from arising as an issue for rational discussion.

It should be stated at once that while the *spirit* of this denial of cognitive status to the sentences of metaphysics and theology still persists, even for some who would

not accept the title of "positivist," the verifiability criterion is no longer recognized
by all contemporary linguistic empiricists
as a norm. For a variety of reasons, original positivism could not sustain itself. The
main difficulty was that of finding a pro-
perly authoritative status for the meaning
criterion itself. It could not be declared
true in its own terms, since it cannot itself
be verified, and yet as a mere stipulation
or rule for language, it fails to have sufficient authority. Moreover, the criterion eliminated too much of the established conceptual structure of natural science to be
finally acceptable. These and other diffi-
culties led to the modification of the original strong formulation of the positivist
position; a weaker criterion was proposed,
dependent on the idea of falsifiability—a
meaningful statement is one for which we
can specify what state of affairs would ren-
der it false. Even this formulation, however, when applied, still retains two fundamental assumptions of the positivist view,
namely that the "basic" or "original"
function of language is to state "facts" and

that such facts are identical with singular sense perceptions recorded by an individual percipient. The first of these assumptions was to be challenged by other linguistic empiricists, while the second has become the target of pragmatists, existentialists and those pursuing the method of phenomenology.

Other developments in the analysis of language, due largely to the influence of G. E. Moore and Wittgenstein, led to innovations that were to have important consequences for the treatment of religious language from the standpoint of linguistic empiricism. Positivism, especially in its continental form, made the languages of formal logic, of mathematics and of physics into ideal models for judging the structure and function of all language. The early Wittgenstein followed this pattern, but he expressed himself in a way that suggested a deeper understanding of the truth. His idea that language "pictures" the facts gave promise of something more subtle to come. Moore had earlier argued that the use of language in ordinary human situations and experience is not to be identified with the use to be encountered in technical or artificial languages developed for special purposes. Moore wanted to preserve the meanings enshrined in ordinary language and his philosophical analyses helped to establish the thesis that the languages of logic and of the natural sciences are not the models for language as such. In this regard, Moore was an opponent of all forms of positivism. Unhappily, his own standard of "ordinary language" had its own restrictions. In laying great stress on what people generally or usually mean by the language they use to conduct business in the daily round, the hard core of ordinary meaning was made the standard for judging non-ordinary — for example, the philosophical — use of terms. Despite Moore's positive contributions to the liberalizing of the linguistic approach to experience, his analyses had the disadvantage that they substituted the confining legislation of common sense, so-called, for the equally confining legislation of the laboratory. If Russell paid too much attention to the language of logicians and mathematicians, Moore was too concerned about what people "ordinarily mean" when they use language; neither model leaves much room for either philosophy or religion. For both involve language that is bound to appear "strange" from the ordinary standpoint, despite the fact that they deal with problems that are faced by every human being.

In a way that is not at all evident, Wittgenstein grasped the situation firmly and suggested that language may actually be *used* in more ways than can be understood if attention were restricted to a standard criterion for *meaning*. As a result, he developed the view that there are many "language games" or uses of language and that each game is determined in structure and import by the *context* and the *purpose* for which it is used. The crucial point is that Wittgenstein was pointing to a more empirical approach to the language situation, one more sensitive to what actually happens in the many circumstances of life where language is used. The experiential turn here was two-fold. First, Wittgenstein advocated a more empirical approach to language itself; previous philosophers had thought primarily of constructing languages out of primitive elements and formation rules, whereas he was directing attention to natural language in actual use— the giving of orders, praying, cursing, translating, handing down legal decisions, greeting friends and indeed all of the functions that belong to human life—and to what happens in such situations. This new approach meant that knowledge of the context of a statement—its function in achieving a certain end—became a necessary condition for determining meaning. Syntax, or the rules for forming compound expressions, does not suffice for this purpose. Secondly, in addition to the more empirical approach to language as such, Wittgenstein was placing emphasis on languages which are themselves richer in experiential content than formal languages can ever be. In short, even if we have doubts, as I do, about the adequacy of dealing with experience solely in terms of language, Wittgenstein struck a blow in

favor of languages deeply rooted in experience. He opened the way for a wider
linguistic empiricism in which the full
range of our encounter with ourselves and
the world can be preserved, or at least as
much of it as has already found expression
in language. Among other things, the influence of the later Wittgenstein was felt
mainly in a shift from exclusive concern
with the language of logic to interest in
discovering what has come to be called the
logic of a given language—art, law, religion, ethics among others.

With this background in mind, let us
now consider some bearings of these developments on religion and especially on
the problem of God. There are three focal
points in the discussion. First, insofar as
linguistic empiricists fully accept and apply the verifiability criterion of meaning
in its strong form, the only possible consequence for theology is that theological
statements in which the term "God" occurs
are meaningless or cognitively vacuous,
even if they retain "emotive" meaning in
some sense. As we have seen, however, not

many philosophers at present would up-
hold the positivist criterion in its original
formulation, although it is clear that the
falsifiability version of the criterion is still
being invoked by linguistic empiricists
when they demand to know what fact or
facts there are in the sensible world that
would count against, or falsify, the proposition "God exists."[10] Curiously e n o u g h,
some contemporary theologians under the
impression that linguistic empiricism represents *the* voice of philosophy, accept the
criterion and declare that "God talk" is
literally meaningless and that consequently, "God is dead." But many philosophers
do not go this far and indeed some at present are even attempting to rehabilitate
the ontological argument. This development, however, does not much affect linguistic empiricists who are generally wary
of abstract logic and remain wedded to
their version of empiricism.

When the problem of God is cast as an
"empirical problem" even for the broader
minded linguistic empiricists, God's reality
is understood as a matter of confirming or

disconfirming an empirical hypothesis in the sense that to claim God's existence is to claim that there is an actual or possible sense perception at the basis of the claim. Two responses are possible for the theologian under these circumstances; he may accept the demand and try to specify what the confirming or disconfirming evidence would be in the next life, or he may refuse to accept the demand on the ground that God's existence, while not without relation to experience, is not correctly interpreted as an empirical hypothesis of the sort that deals with some limited aspect of experience. God is either necessary or impossible; there is no third alternative, with the exception of the claim (which joins the issue at a different point) that the term "God" is without meaning. And as has been pointed out, no one can claim that the idea of God is meaningless on the basis of the original positivist criterion, for that criterion is a dogma without support. Moreover, thinking of God as a reality which may or may not exist is not to think of a reality that could consistently be meant by the term "God" when used in the religious context or language game. Refusing the demand of linguistic empiricism to specify what fact would count against God, is the only sound alternative for theologians to take. Contrary to what has generally been supposed, specifying in terms of particular fact what would confirm or disconfirm the "hypothesis" of God requires more insight into, and certainty about, the divine nature than human beings can command, and more than sense-bound empiricists should be prepared to claim. The point is that there is no non-dogmatic way of declaring discourse about "God" meaningless and therefore linguistic empiricists, among o t h e r philosophers, should either ignore the entire topic or be prepared to consider it in its own terms and not assimilate it to the discussion of an empirical hypothesis.

Secondly, if we follow the Wittgenstein of the later writings, new and more fruitful possibilities of relation between theology and linguistic empiricism are o p e n e d. Much depends upon how the concept of many language games is interpreted, and to what extent Wittgenstein's proposed dissolution of metaphysical questions as due to the "bewitchment" of language remains in force. The two considerations are closely connected. With regard to the latter, it is necessary to understand the ambiguity of the appeal to so-called ordinary l a n g u a g e and experience. On the one hand, the appeal has had the effect of challenging the authority of the formal languages and especially the language of physics as models for all uses of language. By contrast, ordinary language is concrete and experience-laden. On the other hand, ordinary language can be made to exercise a restrictive authority of its own in the sense that metaphysical analysis is condemned as "misleading" because it employs the terms of ordinary language in ways that are illegitimate. Thus it is claimed that with regard to object words of ordinary language such as "camel" and "sphere," we can significantly ask, "What is a camel?" or "What is a sphere?," but that we make a logical blunder if we suppose that we can ask these same questions about "time" or "existence" and expect to receive a similar sort of answer. The appeal to the authority of ordinary language, or to what people ordinarily say, at this point is as dogmatic in the end as was the original positivist meaning criterion; the appeal blocks the road of inquiry. For if there actually are many language games, and each is legitimate in its own way, there is no reason why the languages of metaphysics and theology should be singled out for elimination. Moreover, ordinary language is itself one of the l a n g u a g e games, and it is not obvious why it should become the standard for judging all the others. Metaphysical and theological analysis must remain responsive to, and must not contradict, the experience expressed in and through ordinary language, but that language is not itself the final criterion on all matters of fact and existence. Languages developed in particular contexts for expressing the many different dimensions of what there is have criteria of their own for consistency and critical appraisal. It is a signal fact of our present cultural situation that no one seriously proposes to make ordinary language the criterion for judging the language of natural science (what, for example, is the "ordinary" meaning of "atom," "gene," etc., and why would an answer, if one were forthcoming, be irrelevant?), whereas both metaphysics and theology are often subjected to such judgment. There is no rationality here; it is largely a mark of the present climate of opinion in which science is accepted without criticism and reflective inquiry is subject to an infinite skepticism which, if carried out consistently, would invalidate all rational discourse whatever.

A more fruitful line of inquiry would seem to follow from Wittgenstein's claim that t h e r e actually are many language games and that, using them as guides, we should return to experience in order to "see" all that is there, attending carefully to the way particular languages function when they are actually *used*. This way of approach opens up genuinely interesting and important questions in connection with the religious function of language as, for example, whether the term "God" can be said to function exclusively either as a name or as a description; whether, and how, human response—"conviction," "faith"—enters into the meaning of religious terminology; how the different forms or styles of expression *within* the universe of religious language — myth, parable, legend, prayer, confession, lamentation, hymn, etc.—are related to each other, and especially in what way the more elemental language of religion is related to the conceptualized and systematized language of theology. The linguistic approach is most valuable when it focuses questions of this sort and helps us to avoid confusions stemming from differences of meaning that are obscured by grammatical similarity. A question such as, "Did the Resurrection occur?" has the same grammatical form as the question "Did the death of Churchill occur?" but, whereas the latter question can be answered in a straightforward way, as we say, the former question cannot. The reason for the difference is that the term

"Resurrection" belongs to religious and theological language; it expresses a certain interpretation and belief about the import of Jesus as Christ when used as religious language; as such, the term does not denote a "bare" fact that might have been observed or verified as in the case of the death of a human individual. Analysis of this sort greatly helps to focus issues and sets us on the track of discovering how a term like "Resurrection" does function in actual use. We are led to ask what the belief means to the individual Christian in his personal life and what bearing it may have on the total life of the culture in which he lives. We are also led back to the historical matrix from which the idea of a Being not overcome by death first arose, in order to understand the import of the claim.

Linguistic empiricism by itself, however, does not take us beyond the locating or focusing of issues; it embraces, by definition, no explicit general theory of experience—unless it be a form of positivism and the theory that experience is composed

of atomic sense data that are just what
they are in themselves, essentially unre-
lated to each other and devoid of either
value or tendency. This position, therefore, is unable to deal with the problem of
relating the many different dimensions of
experience to each other. The result is in-
evitable for a philosophy whose aim is
not to add anything to what we already
know or believe that we know, but only to
"clarify," by analysis of language, whatever meaning and experience have already
found expression through that language.
And yet this is not the whole story, for
linguistic empiricists do not confine their
activity to clarification of what other
people—"believers" in the case of religious
language—mean; there are metaphysical
principles operative in their interpretation
and these become evident at the point
where we are told what a given expression
could possibly mean, or *would have to
mean* in order to be intelligible, cognitive,
in accord with ordinary use, etc. At this
point, we are taken beyond what people
actually using the religious language *do*

mean, or are trying to express, or want to
express; we are confronted instead with
the application of a normative criterion
governing what can legitimately be meant.
Here the underlying rationalism of linguistic empiricism becomes clear. Instead
of going back to experience to discover
what people actually *encounter*—as indeed
the later Wittgenstein recommended, except that, for him, the situation of
encounter is always to be approached
through what is *said*—there is an insistence
upon definitions, rules, and the invocation
of criteria which *filter* experience and force
it into predetermined patterns. Linguistic
empiricism cannot resolve the fundamental
problem which it generates because of its
refusal to return to a full scale examination
of experience. Linguistic empiricism is not
reflective enough, a point which brings us
to the third and final focal point concerning its bearings on religion.

There is a basic fact about linguistic
empiricism which may be obscured by the
claim that in following its approach, one
is merely "doing analysis" or "clarifying"

the uses of language. The fact is that the standpoint from which such philosophy is "done," is neither neutral nor semantically vacuous with regard to philosophical suppositions and theses. There is a surprising failure on the part of many contemporary theologians to appreciate this point. The differential character of the linguistic approach can be seen in two ways. First, the philosophical considerations which it makes normative for analysis—for example, the distinction between analytic and synthetic statements, the thesis that necessity is wholly a function of conventional meanings and has no internal connection with existence which is entirely contingent — have been developed largely from analysis that excludes the religious dimension of experience. The logical tools used for the analysis of religious language have been developed largely on the basis of analyzing scientific statements and judgments of ordinary experience. This fact helps to explain the prevalent view that religious language is, *vis a vis* the "straightforward" use of language, *queer*. It is difficult to

see how religious language could appear
otherwise when judged in accordance
with criteria arrived at precisely by ignor-
ing the religious dimension of experience.

A philosophical interpretation should
be responsive to all available sources of
encounter, so that the framing of philosophical prescriptions for the interpretation
of experience will not be one-sided in their
import. There is no reason why the massive
and pervasive fact of religion in all times
and cultures, should not itself contribute
to the formation of a philosophical standpoint from which experience is understood. Linguistic empiricists seem almost
invariably to overlook this point; they
develop distinctions and criteria for the
analysis of language from every source
except religion and then apply these criteria to religious language, only to emerge
with the conclusion that such language is
"odd."

The differential character of linguistic
empiricism shows itself in another way
that has to do not only with language but
with the nature of existence as such. For

many contemporary empiricists, it is an
axiom that a statement purporting to be
"necessary" is *ipso facto* not about existence or experience but is merely explica-
tive of stipulated meanings, while a statement purporting to be about existence or
experience is *ipso facto* not necessary. It
is, of course, precisely this dogma that is
being called into question by the renewed
discussion of the Ontological Argument
for God. That argument claims that there
is, in the assertion of the divine existence,
an example of a necessary statement which
is more than an explication of conventional
meanings and yet is about existence. At
present it is extremely difficult to bring
about an open dialectical consideration of
the doctrine in question because of the
view that all philosophical questions must
be approached from the "empirical" standpoint if we are to arrive at critical results.
But then, being "empirical" requires
adopting the very separation of necessity
and existence which is in question. The
paradoxical character of the situation
points us in the requisite direction; what is

called for is a fundamental examination of
the nature of experience, what it is and
how it discloses reality. For only confusion
can result from the claim that our rational
constructions are based upon, and judged
by, experience, when it is not at all clear
what is meant by *experience*. The great
merit of the third position we are to consider, that of pragmatic empiricism, is that
it made a new beginning with regard to
experience; it is the bearing of that new
beginning upon religion that we seek to
discover.

III. Religion and Pragmatic Empiricism[11]

In discussing the approach to experience developed on the American scene, I
want to begin with an account of the
general shape of experience as envisaged
by such thinkers as Peirce, James and
Dewey, and then go on to illustrate the
relevance of this view for religion by showing how the problem of God can be recast
in terms of experience radically interpreted. It will be helpful if we do not think in
this connection primarily of "pragmatism"

and associated ideas—"practical," "man-made truth," "success," etc., but rather of the reconstruction of experience which the pragmatic philosophers attempted. I believe that there are untapped resources for interpreting religion in the broader and richer view of experience developed by the classical American philosophers. Therefore in the final portion of this discussion, I aim to pass beyond expositions and appraisals to constructive interpretation showing how religion can be experientially understood.

It is out of the question to deal individually and in detail with the theory of experience as expressed by the three thinkers mentioned. Each had his own characteristic approach and opinions, but there is a consensus among them with regard to the general shape of experience and to that we must direct attention. Each thinker, moreover, treated the topic of religion in his own way and their theories are not unimportant. Instead, however, of focusing on these interpretations, I want to consider the wider question of the resources present in the reconstructed theory of experience for a fresh consideration of the problem of God.

The first point is that experience is understood as the record and result of complex interactions and transactions between the human organism or language-using animal and the environment in which that organism lives and moves. As such, experience is *not* primarily a set of mental phenomena immediately present and open to the intuitive inspection of a private mind. It follows that experience is not a screen or veil that stands between the one who experiences and the so-called "external world." Experience is, instead, a valid medium of disclosure through which we come to know what there is. As Dewey expressed it, experience reaches down into nature, revealing the traits and characters of things; experience is not a private and immediately certain film-sequence of phenomena disconnected from the world we encounter. There is, of course, the problem of objectivity and of critical experience, but this problem does not concern the attempted transition from "experience," taken as intuitively certain data of sense, to an "external world" wholly beyond our ken. The point is that we do not begin in the first instance with private certainty and then seek to reach a totally problematic external world by a process of inference. That view makes of experience a veil which we must transcend, whereas experience, on the radical view, is itself the transcendence to nature. To experience at all is to take part in a process of disclosure of a content that is beyond the individual. Objectivity, or experience that will stand criticism, is attained through a critical process of sifting what we encounter and of judging it; attaining critical results depends upon dealing with the materials of experience in a critical way, not upon a dubious leap from private, mental content to an unknown external world.

Closely related to the denial that experience is primarily a private, mental content, is the claim that experience cannot be totally identified with *sense* after the fashion of those who seek the "given"

in the form of the most primitive and unin-
terpreted data of sensation. According to
Dewey's account, we are never in a position to *start* with the given; we begin, instead, *in medias res* and "take," from a
situation that transcends us in every direction, those items that arrest us by their
problematic character. Thought is present
in experience from the beginning. We are
able to reach what was there or "given"
in the first instance, only if we engage in
a painstaking critical process of inquiry
started by the problem that first caught
our attention. The point is that the recovery of the given is never a matter of reaching bare, sensible data. Of the three pragmatists, James came closest to retaining
the traditional connection between experience and sense, although even he argued
vigorously against the view that experience
is composed of clearly demarcated, singular, data. The clear and disconnected impressions of Hume, James regarded as
selections or abstractions from the stream
of experience which is essentially continuous and inclusive of relations.

Peirce and Dewey were no less definite in their rejection of the widely held view that experience means the singular, the sensible, and the immediately present. Peirce argued that experience is inclusive of generality and of tendency or direction, and Dewey claimed that, unless it included an inferential process, experience would be reduced to inarticulate, static and atomic states. The extent to which experience is thought to pass beyond atomic, sensible particulars for these thinkers, can be summed up in two respects—we may call them *context* and *tendency*.

With regard to the former, experience is not merely disclosure of the world's content, but it also reflects the many ways in which reality can be approached. The being who experiences not only has purposes of his own in approaching the world and himself, but he is capable of seeing both in many different *contexts*. It is possible to explain things, to appreciate them, to make them, to transform them, to buy and sell them, to interpret them, etc. In short, the esthetic, the scientific, the economic, the _everybody_

ethical, the religious, all belong to experience. Context and dimension of meaning,
therefore, are inseparable from experience;
we come to know not only *what* is there,
but we understand the things encountered
many times over in different universes of
meaning. Experience includes frameworks
for interpreting as well as that which is
to be interpreted.

With regard to tendency, the main
point is that the contents of experience are
not static units of sensible quality occupy-
ing a present moment of time. In our actual experiencing, we are aware of dis-
criminable items, to be sure, but we are
also aware of their flowing into each
other, of clustering together or of succeed-
ing each other in various purposeful patterns. The continuity and directionality of
experience can be made the object of explicit attention, although we are by no
means always attending to either. If experience is decomposed into static units
no one of these units, taken all by itself,
can indicate the direction or tendency of
the process in which it is involved. But

insofar as experience is itself a process which takes a time, it must embrace both tendency and direction. These relational features are not apprehended as shapes, colors, odors, etc., are apprehended and yet we distort experience if we omit them. Their "cash value," as James would have said, can best be realized in an imaginative construction of our experience. If we plan a series of activities aimed at reaching a certain goal, and perform what Dewey called the "dramatic rehearsal in imagination," we feel that each planned step follows the last in one continuous movement of images. We connect the realized goal of the process with the projected plan, the end with the beginning. Such imaginative experience of what will utimately become sensible movements in the public world of action, is possible only because the material of experience has a structure not sensed in precisely the way in which the contents of experience are sensed.

In addition to denying that experience must be essentially subjective, and that it can be identified with the deliverances of the senses, our pragmatists denied that experience is wholly, or even primarly a matter of theoretical knowledge. Experience, that is, is not essentially the passive observation of phenomena required for scientific endeavor. We participate in experience, we suffer and undergo, we enjoy, appreciate, and live in our experience. We do not exist merely to look at what we encounter or to occupy the role of theoretical observers; instead, we see ourselves taking part in things and we regard the world as the scene of our self-realization. In short, since we are human beings, we are involved and concerned. As Dewey put it, experience is poignant or dull, tragic or triumphant, unsettling or comforting, joyous or frustrating. These complex qualities and meanings belong to experience itself; they are not merely subjective or emotional additions made by the mind to experience. So to judge them is an error that follows from supposing that experience is no richer than the abstract content required for the purpose of theoretical knowledge.

It should now be evident that experience, radically conceived, can be related to religion in a more intimate and fruitful way than was possible with previous forms of empiricism. In attacking the subjectivist conception, and in defending experience as a valid medium of disclosure, the pragmatic philosophers have opened the way to a fresh consideration of God in experiential terms. I do not mean to return to "religious experience," but rather the disclosure of what I would call the "religious dimension" of experience. This dimension of our dealings with reality gives rise to the question of God, or of an ultimate ground for our existence. Dogmatic theologians of all persuasions have invariably rejected the appeal to experience in the belief that experience is no more than a tissue of subjectivity. In this they have confused the idea of God with God as an actual ingredient in experience. For God must be a living power over and above all ideas. When theologians deny experience, they are guilty of abandoning it to those who reduce it to the abstract material of

theoretical knowledge. But if experience,
in its full depth and scope, is an objective
result of man's transactions with the total
environment, including himself, the relevance of experience for religion and theology becomes important indeed. The contrast between the "objectivity" of doctrine
rooted in tradition and expressed in syste-
matic form, and the "subjectivity" of experience taken to be the feeling content of
a private consciousness, rests on a great
mistake. For by contrast with experience
understood as a critical and publicly available result, *all* doctrine, including the doctrine of God, is abstract and incomplete.

In attacking the view that experience
is the same as sensible content, the pragmatic empiricists have opened a way to an
understanding of transcendence. Dogmatic
theologians have often believed that the
case is precisely the opposite on the ground
that experience precludes, in principle, the
possibility of divine transcendence. The
belief has been that man's experience is
merely finite in contrast with the divine,
and that his entire experience is a tissue of

"immanence." There are at least two errors in this supposition. First, there is no good reason to deny that experience is disclosure of a reality transcending the experience of each individual. Experience means whatever is actually encountered in whatever way. The fact that something is disclosed *through* experience does not *ipso facto* transform it into "experience" in the sense of mental representations present only for the immediate consciousness of a spectator. Secondly, the notion of transcendence itself is misunderstood if it is supposed that a reality ingredient or immanent in human experience in some specifiable ways, is thereby wholly identical with or reduced to that ingredience. Even spatio-temporally situated objects have this transcendence, since one and the same such object can be ingredient in the experience of many different individuals and the object clearly cannot be identified with the experience of any one of them. How much more is this true for God who is, by the nature of his Being, related to *all* that exists and happens. The crucial point

is that experience does not imply the total
immanence of any of its ingredients.

If we can overcome the prejudice that
prevents us from taking experience seriously, we shall be in a position to see that
it provides us with that *concreteness*, what
James called the "sense of reality," which
the present religious situation so desper-
ately needs. The fact is that the modern
man has lost God because he does not find
God ingredient in experience or does not
recognize Him where He may be found.
Eager, young theologians at present grasp
this point and set out to find a radically
new understanding of God. Unfortunately,
they seem not to know what experience is,
and, supposing it to be what they have
learned from linguistic empiricism, they
proceed to announce the "death of God."
This conclusion is more consistent than
might at first be supposed, for among the
dead one can find only death. But what
if the error consists in seeking the *living*
among the dead? It seems clear that God,
as living Power, will not be found as one
item among others in the stock of items

recognized by an empiricism that sees experience only in terms of clear-cut, sensible
phenomena forming the material for theoretical knowledge. To this extent the radical theologians are right, but what if God
were ingredient in experience understood
in a new way? The radical or pragmatic
conception of experience opens up this
momentous possibility for us.

Here I leave behind the exposition of
points of view, their relations and respec-
tive merits, in order to mark out the experiential approach to the problem of God
which seems to me the only viable response
to current perplexities about God. I have
tried to follow the trail of empiricism in
modern philosophy and to show the influence of that development on religion. I
believe that only the pragmatic or radical
view of experience is adequate for making
sense out of religion in experiential terms.
Thus far I have indicated some of the vir-
tues of the radical position in essentially
general or abstract terms; it is now time to
stop talking *about* experience and attend
to what we actually experience. The ab-

stract treatment was, however, necessary; there is no point in urging a return to experience when it is widely supposed that experience is necessarily insubstantial and subjective. I shall be guided by the *spirit* of James, of Peirce and of Dewey, but the *letter* will be my own. They opened a way, and we must learn from them, but they did not face precisely our situation, and therefore we cannot solve our problems by reviving their solutions.

To speak to the contemporary religious situation it is necessary as a first step to understand the mood and attitude of the modern man. He may be indifferent, hostile, skeptical in the face of religion, but he is, above all else, confused, hesitant, and without adequate understanding. No matter how many enigmas religion has been supposed in the past to solve, the fact is that religion today has itself become an enigma. Surveying the landscape as candidly as possible, most people, whether officially "religious" or not, do not find God in their sights, and they do not clearly see what place in their experience God would fill. For many there is the strong sense that hypocrisy is worse than the loss of God; there is a widespread refusal to continue repeating the formulas of traditional relig- ion without any clear understanding of their meaning. The refusal is a good sign, as long as it is accompanied with openness and a continuing interest in finding the truth. Unfortunately, the spokesmen for religion have not always been helpful at this point; they have too often taken the resistance of the modern man for a hostile rejection of God, thus failing to understand the possibilities inherent in a situation where people really care enough to refuse to say they understand what they do not understand, or to see what they do not see. The only useful response is to set aside superior claims to truth and revelation and start with man's situation in the world; from that vantage point we must seek to grasp what religion is and means. Here we are; no one of us, as Kierkegaard has well said, was consulted about being here, and no one of us can avoid—except by the desperate act of self-annihilation — t h e questioning, the puzzling, the striving to discover who we are, why we are, and what the whole thing means.

If we attend carefully to our situation in the world, we know that, like men in all times and places, we question the *from whence* of our life and the *to whence* of our striving. In short, we raise the question and have a concern about the ultimate boundaries of our being. If we are actually guided by the thread of our experience, we see that the *problem* of God as the Ground and Goal of our life and indeed of all existence, precedes the assertion of God. Most men puzzle about God, before they accept Him. Unfortunately, this order has often been reversed. The defenders of religious traditions have invariably presented us with the assertion of God, with the guarantee of the divine reality, long before we have clearly grasped the problem of God, and too often we have accepted the assertion as a matter of course only to reject it later when the full impact of the problem of God has come upon us. Experience suggests that we should make a new start and

begin with the problem of God as it arises
in the life of every man. The problem belongs to man's life in the world; it will not
do to suppose that some people start out
with the assurance of God, while others
confront only a problem. *All* men, including, or perhaps one should say, especially,
those who have faith in God, confront God
as a problem. The man of faith, if his faith
is a living one, has come to his position
through a sea of doubt, a sea which still
surrounds him so that his faith is not a
fixed state, but rather a continual struggle
against the uncertainty that ever threatens
to dislodge his assurance. The failure of
professedly religious people to remain
honestly sensitive to the continuing doubts
that assail them has had the effect of cut-
ting them off from other men, and of ob-
scuring the force of God as a problem. The
fact is that the assurance of God always
exists on the far side of uncertainty. This
fact is hidden from us when we approach
religion in a non-experiential way, supposing that it means no more than proclaiming the reality of God guaranteed in ad-

vance through a tradition, without first
setting forth the problem of God as it
arises in our encounter with the world and
ourselves.

The problem of God arises out of the
religious dimension of experience. Experience has, as we have seen, contexts or
dimensions as well as content. The religious dimension comes into view when we
encounter in our own selves a peculiar
question and concern, the question and
concern for the quality of our life and our
world *taken as a whole.* We are aware of
problems, questions, perplexities, anxieties
in connection with specific and limited
areas and aspects of our life, and experience acquaints us with the fact that there
are problematic situations *in* life. In en-
countering ourselves, however, and in re-
flecting on the fact of our being in the
world at all, we come to realize that our
total life is problematic in the sense that
we stand in need of a purpose for being, a
self-integrating power that makes self-
realization possible in a situation constant-
ly threatening us both from without and

from within. The problem of the self-integrating power *is* the problem of God cast in experiential form. In experience we discover not only that there are problems *in* life, but that there is a problem *of* life—the problem of finding an ultimate object of devotion integrating and unifying t h e many powers and potentialities of our personal being. The religious dimension of experience is the one in which man asks the question and experiences the concern for the ground and goal of his life as a whole. Both aspects are essential, both question and concern. Question points to the reflective idea arising within us, the idea of a supreme object of devotion by which we orient ourselves; concern points to the fact that the question is about the being of the one who asks the question. We stand in *need* of the object of devotion for the realization of ourselves and for the transformation of ourselves. Our quest is not for *information* or knowledge alone, but for *inspiration* or the power to shape our lives in accordance with an ideal.

The problem of God—the problem of
What or Who is the Ground of our being
and of all existence and where that reality
is to be found—is generated by man's encounter with the world and himself. Instead of beginning, as we sometimes have
done, with a fully developed doctrine of
God, we should begin with the origin of
the question of God in experience which
all men share. This does not mean that
doctrine is unnecessary, but rather that we
cannot begin with it. For to set out with
a fixed doctrine of God, especially one
drawn from an historical religious tradition, gives rise to the belief that God is one
more being among others in the world that
surrounds us. We are led to suppose that
there are three realities—the world and
ourselves with which we are familiar, and
a third reality, "God" with whom we are
not on very clear terms. But this way of
approach cuts us off from a proper understanding of religion which can be gained
only by seeing the sort of problem in man's
existence to which God is the answer. A
ready-made doctrine of God stemming

from an historical religion such as the
Judeo-Christian, represents the faith of a
community that has already found God.
Merely proclaiming the doctrine of this
already-found God to those who do not
clearly understand the question of God, is
like providing a man with answers to questions which he has not yet really asked.
There is time enough for theological reflection and dialectic, *after* the *problem* of
God has been elucidated in experiential
terms and after a person comes to understand that the problematic situation in
which he finds himself is what leads men
to ask for God in the first instance.

The power and importance of the question and concern that constitute the religious dimension of experience appear most
clearly when we consider some of the at-
tempts made by man to resolve his own
problematic situation through his own resources. Some have sought for the ultimate
object of devotion in knowledge, especially
in that knowledge which is science, and
have supposed that devotion to the life of
science and to shaping conduct on the

basis of scientific knowledge, will result in that self-integration which is the goal of the religious quest. Others have found the ultimate object of devotion in the state and they have supposed that finding a proper place in the political and social order and doing one's duty in both spheres provides man with the final purpose of his existence. Still others have appealed to time and history and have envisaged a cosmic progress to which each man can contribute so that he finds the purpose of his existence in the perfecting of things for posterity. Countless other objects, drawn from man's life in the world, have been set up as objects of supreme devotion and thus as sources of salvation, or being made whole. Thus we say, and not without just cause, that men have made a "religion" out of science, or have transformed the state into God. And while it seems to me illegitimate to claim, as some apologists for religion have, that because men behave in this way it shows that all men believe in "God," such behavior does help to elucidate the religious dimension in man's experience. For it shows the ineluctable lure of an object of supreme devotion and the inescapability of man's problematic situation as one who stands in need of a power of self-integration.

We approach the problem of God more closely when we examine the many objects elevated to the status of supreme objects of devotion and discover that they are one and all finite and conditioned realities, completely subject to the structure of existence. As finite, these realities are not themselves self-sustaining and therefore are subject to change and to decay. They are not fitted to remain objects of supreme devotion because they have a finite fate or destiny and are therefore not ultimate. Prometheus, in the ancient myth, has a place of standing over against Zeus who seeks to destroy him, because Zeus, though chief among the gods, is subject to the power of Necessity or Destiny. Beyond Zeus there is a more ultimate reality. So it is with contemporary, finite substitutes for God; they cannot do what they are supposed to do, but they, nevertheless, help us to understand the religious dimension of our experience, and to see the problem of God as the problem of finding the supreme object of devotion which alone has the power to overcome the forces that threaten to undo us.

The experiential reinterpretation of God as the supreme object of devotion and as the self-integrating Power of human existence, does not of itself *resolve* the problem of God in contemporary life. Nor indeed was it supposed to do so. The main point of going back to experience was to confront us with the problem of God by showing what the problem means in the human situation. The pervasive character of man's problematic situation in the world points to the inescapability of the religious dimension. Confronting a problem, however, is not a solution, any more than diagnosis is a cure. But both are necessary beginnings and without them no advance can be made.

NOTES

1. Locke, *An Essay Concerning Human Understanding*, Bk. II. ch. I, 2.

2. Locke, *An Essay Concerning Human Understanding*, Bk. II. ch. XVII.

3. Locke, *An Essay Concerning Human Understanding*, Bk. II. ch. XVII, 6.

4. Locke, *An Essay Concerning Human Understanding*, Bk. IV chs. IX, X.

5. Locke, *An Essay Concerning Human Understanding*, Bk. IV. ch. IX.

6. Hume, *Inquiry Concerning Human Understanding*, Section XII, Part iii.

7. Hume, *Dialogues Concerning Natural Religion*, Part II.

8. See especially the excellent treatment of the entire topic by James A. Martin, Jr., *The New Dialogue Between Philosophy and Theology*, New York: Seabury Press, Inc., 1966. See also the perceptive paper of Fr. W. Norris Clarke, S.J., "Analytic Philosophy and Language About God" in G. F. McLean, ed., *Christian Philosophy and Religious Renewal*, Washington: Catholic University Press, 1966; for the development on the philosophical side, see G. J. Warnock, *English Philosophy Since 1900*, London: Oxford University Press, 1958.

9. A. J. Ayer, *Language, Truth and Logic*, London: W. Gollancz, 1947, p. 115.

10. See, for example, Kai Nielsen, "On Fixing The Reference Range of 'God'" in *Religious Studies*, Vol. 2, No. 1 (1966), pp. 13-36.

11. See especially, Dewey, "The Need for a Recovery of Philosophy" in *Creative Intelligence: Essays in the Pragmatic Attitude,* Dewey, *et al,* New York: H. Holt and Company, 1917; *A Common Faith,* New Haven: Yale University Press, 1934; William James, "A World of Pure Experience" and "The Experience of Activity" in *Essays in Radical Empiricism,* New York: Longmans, Green and Company, 1912, "The Stream of Thought" and "Attention" in *Principles of Psychology,* New York: H. Holt and Company, 1890. Peirce's ideas concerning the meaning of experience are found throughout his many writings; consult *Collected Papers of C. S. Peirce,* Vols. I-VI, ed. Hartshorne and Weiss, Vols. VII, VIII, ed., Burks, Cambridge (Mass.): Harvard University Press, 1931, 1958; also my paper "Religion and Theology in Peirce" in *Studies in the Philosophy of C. S. Peirce,* ed., Wiener and Young, Cambridge (Mass.): Harvard University Press, 1952.

The Aquinas Lectures

Published by the Marquette University Press
Milwaukee, Wisconsin 53233

Cicero in the Courtroom of St. Thomas Aquinas (1945) by E. K. Rand, Ph.D., Litt.D., LL.D., (1871-1945) Pope professor of Latin, *emeritus*, Harvard University.

St. Thomas and Epistemology (1946) by Louis-Marie Regis, O.P., Th.L., Ph.D., director of the Albert the Great Institute of Mediaeval Studies, University of Montreal.

St. Thomas and the Greek Moralists (1947, Spring) by Vernon J. Bourke, Ph.D., professor of philosophy, St. Louis University, St. Louis, Missouri.

History of Philosophy and Philosophical Education (1947, Fall) by Étienne Gilson of the *Académie française*, director of studies and professor of the history of Mediaeval philosophy, Pontifical Institute of Mediaeval Studies, Toronto.

The Natural Desire for God (1948) by William R. O'Connor, S.T.L., Ph.D., former professor of dogmatic theology, St. Joseph's Seminary, Dunwoodie, N.Y.

St. Thomas and the World State (1949) by Robert M. Hutchins, former Chancellor of the University of Chicago, president of the Fund for the Republic.

Method in Metaphysics (1950) by Robert J. Henle, S.J., Ph.D., academic vice-president, St. Louis University, St. Louis, Missouri.

Wisdom and Love in St. Thomas Aquinas (1951) by Étienne Gilson of the *Académie française,* director of studies and professor of the history of Mediaeval philosophy, Pontifical Institute of Mediaeval Studies, Toronto.

The Good in Existential Metaphysics (1952) by Elizabeth G. Salmon, Ph.D., professor of philosophy in the graduate school, Fordham University.

St. Thomas and the Object of Geometry (1953) by Vincent Edward Smith, Ph.D., director, Philosophy of Science Institute, St. John's University.

Realism and Nominalism Revisited (1954) by Henry Veatch, Ph.D., professor and chairman of the department of philosophy, Northwestern University.

Imprudence in St. Thomas Aquinas (1955) by Charles J. O'Neil, Ph.D., professor of philosophy, Villanova University.

The Truth That Frees (1956) by Gerard Smith, S.J., Ph.D., professor and chairman of the department of philosophy, Marquette University.

St. Thomas and the Future of Metaphysics (1957) by Joseph Owens, C.Ss.R., Ph.D., professor of philosophy, Pontifical Institute of Mediaeval Studies, Toronto.

Thomas and the Physics of 1958: A Confrontation (1958) by Henry Margenau, Ph.D.,

Eugene Higgins professor of physics and natural philosophy, Yale University.

Metaphysics and Ideology (1959) by Wm. Oliver Martin, Ph.D., professor of philosophy, University of Rhode Island.

Language, Truth and Poetry (1960) by Victor M. Hamm, Ph.D., professor of English, Marquette University.

Metaphysics and Historicity (1961) by Emil L. Fackenheim, Ph.D., professor of philosophy, University of Toronto.

The Lure of Wisdom (1962) by James D. Collins, Ph.D., professor of philosophy, St. Louis University.

Religion and Art (1963) by Paul Weiss, Ph.D. Sterling professor of philosophy, Yale University.

St. Thomas and Philosophy (1964) by Anton C. Pegis, Ph.D., professor of philosophy, Pontifical Institute of Mediaeval Studies, Toronto.

The University In Process (1965) by John O. Riedl, Ph.D., professor of philosophy, Marquette University.

The Pragmatic Meaning of God (1966) by Robert O. Johann, S.J., associate professor of philosophy, Fordham University.

Uniform format, cover and binding.